A break in Silence

Upasana Chatterjee

BlueRose ONE.com
Stories Matter

First Published in June 2022

ISBN: 978-93-5628-106-6

BLUEROSE PUBLISHERS
www.BlueRoseONE.com
info@bluerosepublishers.com
+91 8882 898 898

Cover Design:
Aveek

Typographic Design:
Rohit

Distributed by: BlueRose, Amazon, Flipkart

Contents

My story, perhaps!

My story is getting told,
These days, in manifold ways.
Dirty talks, raunchy tales,
A battle for custody may be,
Sudden outrage amid all peace.

They found lately a disparity in me.
In my actions, perhaps, and in my destiny
"Why did you do that?" now stands against
"This is what you were supposed to do!"

I had a reason, for sure
That accounts for my fall
The one that Adam had and scared us all
"What did he do to himself" is now a fallacy forever
Doomed he was though, with guilt and awe.

The crescent of the moon

The night seems bloated,
Like swelled-up yeast
My restless eyes
Are ditched by sleep.
The weary world sits
And waits, for what's to come.

Can you see from afar?
Storms up a blizzard
In the blue of my kohl,
Tears rolling toward
My chest and down
Mirroring in each drop
The crescent of the moon.

A deluge gushes downhill,
In an unrestrained flux
Whizzing through the woods,
Ripping up the rocks.
Vain pride thaws loose,
In a demented daze
Only shines all night,
The crescent of the moon.

I waited.

I saw a blackbird once
Flying afar, Shrieking,
Feeling up, maybe, the
Dropping pressure in the air.

Remember looking up the sky?
And gazing at the stars?
With me, lying on this grass?

I returned here again
Long before you would.
I prepared my soul
And tasted it like
The finest wine
I kindled a fire
With scented wood,
And kept the flames
Burning all night.

To keep them alive
I varnished the roses with
The blood from my veins
For a long-lasting stain

I wish I could sing
Some melody to your ears
Or strike up a chord and
Resonate with yours.

It feels like a lifetime now
That I am waiting for you
I waited forever to see my end
Sitting here, beside the pyre.

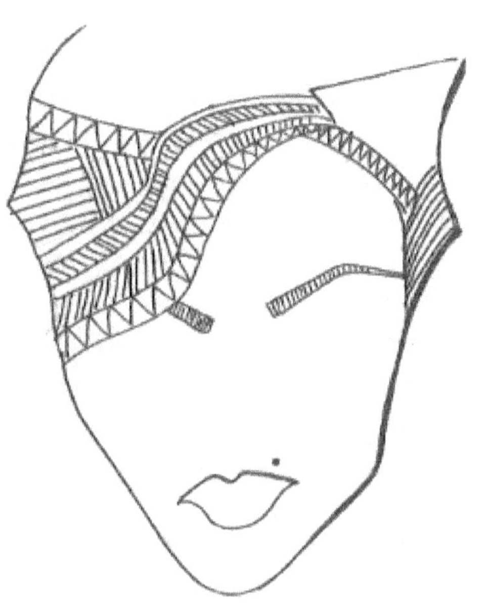

Beauty spot

I don't try to find miracles in you
Anymore,
Nor do I fill my emptiness
Dreaming of you.
No longer wade through backwaters
Devising dire schemes,
To win you back.

I've now set ablaze
What you called my 'beauty spot'
All set to put the town afire,
And crumble down
The stake you upended
To mark my end.

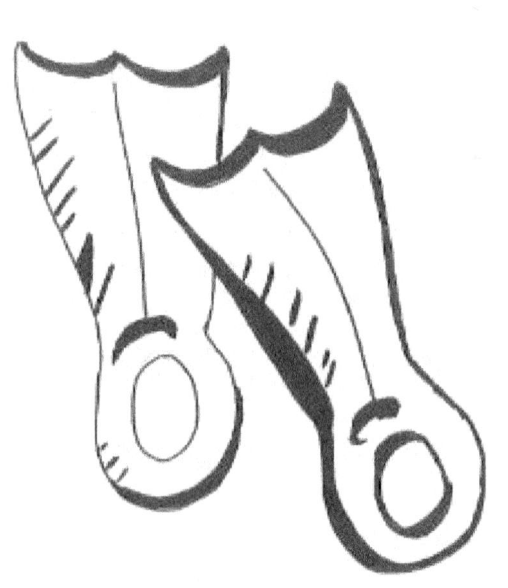

Our waves

We've learned our waves better
Running up and down the shore,
Withstood the pull of tides
Trying to beat the blows.

You chased me along the coast
But never could catch me, though.

I played in the waves, faced down,
Feeling up the force of the highest tide,
Sometimes an unreasonable low.

You sat far away on the golden sand,
All that while, with your fancy flippers on.

A break in silence

A sudden break in silence
Is a longed-for thing
In this space, we inhabit in

Gushes out a faint glow
From the quiet hum.

Sooner or too late,
We'll breathe that gleam
For one more time
We'll sing that hymn
That illuminates surround.

Toxic

From your head to the toe,
You justify every drop of your toxicity

Still, it clings to the brim, thicker than honey
Caustic than vitriol, green to the core
It settles to be there and eat away slow.

Binary & the basics

A binary status lets us know
Our basics, a one and a zero
Takes us through a riddling path.
With replications of code
Our birth-old selfdom
Suddenly looks vain
Versus a fallacy of
Bizarre transmutation.

Sinister percolates
Into that borderline, although
One temptation is there for sure.
Extremities are not obscure
Visions are not opaque anymore.

You regain your pace, ever since,
You again get your basics aligned.

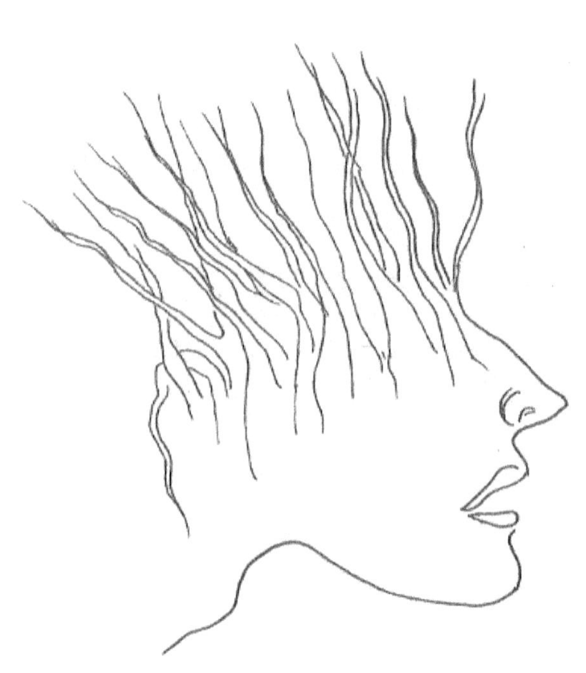

Melting point.

No herb can opiate my bruise
It oozes an ounce of sand
I waited maybe for another
Epileptic assault to bear.

The sea has receded to its depth
To what it's been congenial with.
The coast is dry and barren forever
Retelling the story of birth & death.

Where have I left my days behind,
When I ditched those starry nights?
Or have I lost my eyes to find
Them, in this blinding storm
That's just taken flight.

It has now reached its melting point
The yolk pours off the white of the sky.
Emptying the core,
A stream of magma descends below
Will it shatter that hardest floor?

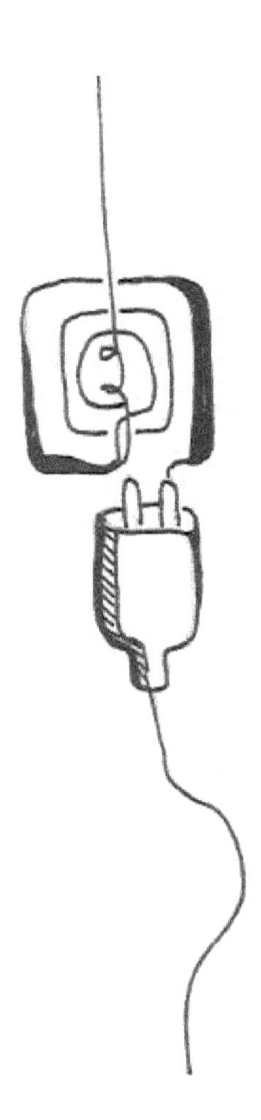

All that matters

When we don't get the newspaper on time
Don't we feel powerless?
Don't we lose our sole obligation
To feel rationally significant?
At least this way we can feign
To bring out our existential plug
And attach it to the power socket
Our mind gets grip on
All things that 'matter'
To rise up and revolt
Against the flow
Our frail actuality
For this pleasant while,
Stays reasonably low.

What could be!

There are a few maybes
That rule our lives
We live in our destiny,
Doomed howsoever,
We still cling on.

Walking along the unchosen,
We often step aside,
Look behind and see,
For once or for twice
What could rather be!

You taught me well!

You're the one who taught me
To lick the sickeningly sweet.
You pushed me up the ladder
From innocence to the facade of it.

Ready for the world, I can win the race,
My victory moves on a spread of chess,
Which table to win over?
Which way does the roulette spin?
You made me a hopeless liar,
Putting up a perfect face!

The thesis of sublime

They still punish at the crossroads
Flogging. In hot savage weather.
Do they have to hide it at all?
In any darkness of silhouette?

No one is here kissing on the lips
Or taking beloveds in an embrace
There'll be no flowing down of water
No thesis of sublime.

Nightmares have broken in
Impotent dreams shattering
Pierced lungs and frameless figures
Crushing smiles from the lips
Slashing songs from bleeding gullets,
Butchers chase with tainted cleavers.

Their breath emits ashes,
Pools of blood dried on the ground
They've perhaps crossed an impasse
A path knowing no end.

Newness

Will you now forget me rather?
And find a new for this old?
A new face to greet you
New delights to cheer at?

You grew on me like a tree
Crept upward, bore fruits and flowers
You said you needed amendments
"And see, Destiny is what you make"!

Will you now daydream, that's
A figment of a feeble brain?
You deserted our songs
Those I shall forget not,
A new tide you may have embarked on
I swim in my silent lake.

My fearless prince

When you find me walking alone
Wading through the sands and shades
You fear to look back at me
In the dismissal of some kind.

Is it only in a night's dream,
That some holy magic shimmers?
Across the cosmic sphere?

You come out brave
As some fearless prince
Hold me tight in your arms
And soothe my bruises
And all my burns.

On the moral scale

Ever been there that is right in the middle?
Of a quiet road and a raging sea,
Or the murky haze in a wintry night?

You gave your best to climb out
Into the numbness from all your pain.
Your nape got crumbled and
Lips pouted in your deepest sleep
Towards those of the depraved.

You wish you pulled out
A ruthless sword with a razor edge.
But one more time they weighed your worth
On the callous measure of the moral scale.

The epilogue of a performance

Look at her, take a closer look
She has returned in greasepaint,
Walking in her shiniest boots,
Precise on swanky floorboards.

Eyes on the glistening trophy,
She heads towards the podium.
A toast for years of winning
Or her relentless forbearance.

Can she smell a chromosomal burnt?
Is she breathing heavy, of late?
She left mascara stain on her pillow,
She must've slept in makeup last night.
Her contour brush went wild on the face
Creating rifts in high cheekbones
Sprite motions are withering away
Can she see her magic decompose?

Stories we heard in a lifetime
Of a temptress or a phantom being
She's walking to the glaring stage,
Telling perhaps her last epilogue.

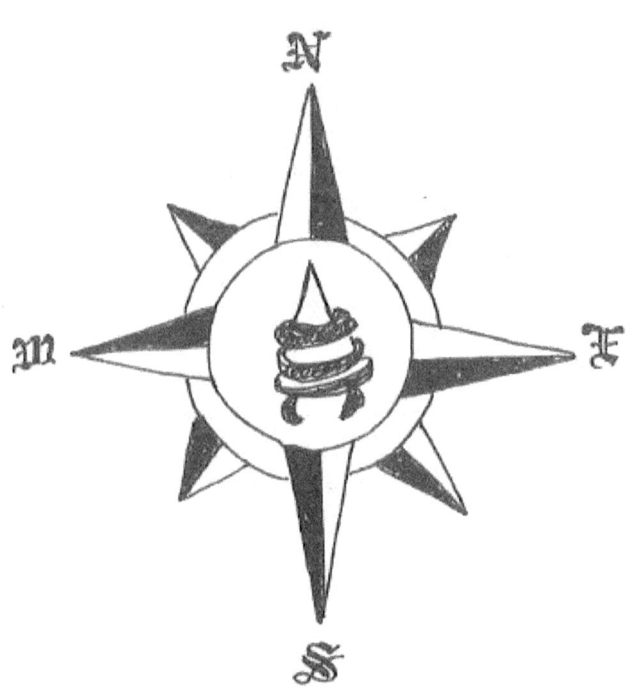

N
W
E
S

Sense of direction

No matter where we go
We carry our darkness with us
Looking for hideaways
We call them homes.

Our eyes adjust often
With our darkness around
We feel the viscosity, over time,
And see through the chasm
We attain a sense of direction.

Guilty pleasure

You too had your guilty pleasures
Much in contrary to your standings

Not sure what is said about you
Some unusual habits, low in regard
Social unacceptability, hostile neighbours

No matter where you go
Without a shadow of a doubt
You too carry
What they call depraved
But you don't
Vices they notice
But you don't.

You carry wherever you go
Your jouissance
A hunger to do what you want.

Every time you tried

Like any conscious sapience
You lusted like some maniac
Your brain got beguiled
When your world fell apart
Held on to everything
You ever could find.

Every time you tried
To rise against the wall
You defended
All that was conflicted
Your wish to show a magic
As an artist
Or a genius of some kind

You dropped and collapsed again.

The morning after

This morning unfurled onto a usual day
Started easy and erased completely
All traces of last night
Blew it away like smoke in the air.

The daylight replaced all that was pleasant
All that was glistening at night
The softness of the music
The gleaming of the light

Who knew that a sinister entity
Was lurking from behind
And designed a doom for the day.

Euphoria

It came down my spines
Midway it stormed up
A euphoria, maybe
Some overwhelming desire.
A sudden blast within.

It didn't make any noise, though
Didn't leave any trace.
My embellished garb came down
On the white of the floor.

Volcano

The Volcano has lost its art of eruption
Sits and waits in a corner
Like some prisoner waiting
For his sentence to come

Four seasons do pass
Some clouds, some rains
Snow covers the tops
Sun melts it once again

Then the blood starts flowing
On the broken stones
It crawls slowly,
Toward the breaches of the bars.

Broken

Have you noticed?
Light breaks
Every time you shatter a glass.

On the broken pieces
I walk on my toes
Picking up the shards

And I strive for my best
To put them together
Will it join like before again
Will the light ever shine?